This Book Belongs to :

Made in the USA
Monee, IL
04 December 2022

19608589R00070